D1733676

THANKSGIVING

by Charles C. Hofer

PEBBLE
a capstone imprint

Published by Pebble, an imprint of Capstone
1710 Roe Crest Drive, North Mankato, Minnesota 56003
capstonepub.com

Library of Congress Cataloging-in-Publication Data is available on the Library of Congress website.
ISBN: 9780756575977 (hardcover)
ISBN: 9780756575922 (paperback)
ISBN: 9780756575939 (ebook PDF)

Summary: Thanksgiving is the day people give thanks for the blessings in their lives. It's also a time to gather with family and friends to enjoy traditional foods like turkey, stuffing, and pumpkin pie. Celebrated on the fourth Thursday in November, this American holiday has been around since the 1620s. From the very first celebration to today's parades, food, and football, learn about this festive holiday's traditions and history.

Editorial Credits
Editor: Alison Deering; Designer: Jaime Willems; Media Researcher: Rebekah Hubstenberger; Production Specialist: Whitney Schaefer

Image Credits
Alamy: North Wind Picture Archives, 10; Getty Images: Andrew Burton, 12, Chip Somodevilla, 23, Helen H. Richardson/The Denver Post, 21, Jose Luis Pelaez Inc, 15, National Archives, 13, Photos.com, 9, Shestock, 18, skynesher, 1, 29; Shutterstock: Alexander Raths, cover, Argentarius, 26, Elena Veselova, 5, Ganeshkumar Durai, 20, JeniFoto, 19, kazoka, 27, Nancy Anderson, 6, PeopleImages.com - Yuri A, 16, Rawpixel.com, 25, STEKLO, 7, Steve Cukrov, 17, Thanaphong Araveeporn, 11

Design Elements
Shutterstock: Rafal Kulik

TABLE OF CONTENTS

Words in **bold** are in the glossary.

TIME TO GIVE THANKS

Summer is over. Winter is coming. The table is full of yummy food. There is turkey for dinner. There's pumpkin pie for dessert.

Family is here. Friends are gathered too. It's time to give thanks for all that we have. It's time to celebrate Thanksgiving!

Thanksgiving is a holiday that is full of **traditions**. It always takes place in the fall. It's time to give thanks for the **harvest** and all the food it brings.

Many countries around the world celebrate during this time of year. Thanksgiving is a **national** holiday in the United States. It is celebrated on the fourth Thursday of November.

THE HISTORY OF THANKSGIVING

Thanksgiving is an important part of United States history. It started before the U.S. was even a country.

In 1620, a group of people left England and came to North America. They later became known as the **Pilgrims.** They landed in what would become Massachusetts.

Life was very hard at first. There wasn't enough food. The wild lands were full of dangers.

The Pilgrims set sail from England.

Squanto helped the Pilgrims
learn how to survive.

In 1621, the Pilgrims met a Native man named Squanto. He introduced them to a local group of Native people called the Wampanoag. They taught the Pilgrims how to catch fish. They also taught them how to grow food like corn.

Soon, the Pilgrims had enough to eat. They shared a **feast** with the Native people. This celebration would become the first Thanksgiving.

The feast soon became an American tradition. In 1789, President George Washington announced a day of national thanksgiving and prayer. In 1863, President Abraham Lincoln made the last Thursday of November Thanksgiving Day.

President Franklin D. Roosevelt changed the date in 1941. He signed a law saying Thanksgiving would always be on the fourth Thursday in November. The holiday has been celebrated on that day ever since.

President Franklin D. Roosevelt

THANKSGIVING TRADITIONS

Thanksgiving is a special holiday. It is all about spending time with friends and family. The holiday also comes with fun traditions. One is eating lots of yummy food!

Thanksgiving dinner today is very different than it was for the Pilgrims. No one knows for sure what they ate. There might have been deer, corn, and shellfish. Today, the main food for most people is turkey. This tasty bird is filled with delicious stuffing.

Thanksgiving has plenty of side dishes too. Many people like cranberry sauce, green beans, mashed potatoes, and gravy. Yum! There's so much to eat for Thanksgiving dinner.

Dessert is also an important
part of the meal. Pumpkin pie is
a Thanksgiving favorite. Apple
pie and pecan pie are popular too.
Sweet potato pie is on the table
in many Southern states.

Thanksgiving isn't just about eating. There are other traditions too. It can be a fun time for arts and crafts. Try drawing a fun turkey by tracing your hand. Give the bird colorful feathers.

Another Thanksgiving tradition is making a **cornucopia**. This "horn of plenty" is a **symbol**. It represents the harvest and other things to be thankful for. It makes a beautiful decoration for the Thanksgiving dinner table.

a cornucopia

Many cities host Thanksgiving **parades**. Giant balloons of cartoon characters float down the street. Thousands of people come out to watch.

A float from the Thanksgiving Day parade in Chicago, Illinois

People take off running in a
Turkey Trot race in Denver, Colorado.

Some cities also host a race called a Turkey Trot. It takes place before the big Thanksgiving dinner. Some people dress up in silly costumes.

Football is a big Thanksgiving tradition for some families. There are three different matchups on TV. People gather to watch the big games.

Thanksgiving has some **unique** traditions too. Each year the president of the United States **pardons** at least one turkey. This takes place on the front lawn of the **White House**.

This tradition officially started in 1989. President George H.W. Bush pardoned the first turkey. It has been happening ever since.

President Barack Obama
pardons a turkey.

OTHER CELEBRATIONS

Other countries celebrate Thanksgiving in different ways. Canada has its own Thanksgiving. It falls on the second Monday in October. The holiday honors some of the first people to explore Canada.

People gather with friends and family to give thanks. Holiday meals are similar to American Thanksgiving. People eat turkey, ham, roast beef, and more.

Football is also a tradition. The Canadian Football League airs its Thanksgiving Day Classic.

Germany and some other countries celebrate Erntedankfest. It takes place in September or October. It is a religious festival. It is also a time to celebrate the harvest. There are parades, music, and dancing.

Erntedankfest celebrates the harvest.

Japanese farmers enjoy
a good harvest.

People in Japan celebrate Kinro Kansha no Hi. The name means Labor Thanksgiving Day. It's a day to give thanks for all the hard work done during the year. It is a quiet holiday. Families celebrate with dinner together.

Thanksgiving marks the start of the holiday season. Other celebrations soon follow. Christmas and Hanukkah come next. They are followed by Kwanzaa and New Year's Day. It is a fun time of year.

No matter where you live, Thanksgiving is a special holiday. It is a time to be with friends and family. It's a day to be thankful for all that we have.

GLOSSARY

cornucopia (kor-nuh-KOH-pee-uh)—a horn-shaped container for food; the cornucopia is a symbol of plenty

feast (FEEST)—to eat a large meal; a large, fancy meal for a lot of people on a special occasion

harvest (HAR-vist)—to gather crops that are ripe; harvest can also be the crops that are gathered

national (NASH-uh-nuhl)—to do with or belonging to a country as a whole

parade (puh-RADE)—a line of people, bands, cars, and floats that travels through a town; parades celebrate special events and holidays

pardon (PAHR-duhn)—an act of official forgiveness

Pilgrims (PIL-gruhms)—the people who left England, came to North America for religious freedom, and founded Plymouth Colony in 1620

symbol (SIM-buhl)—a design or object that stands for something else

tradition (truh-DISH-uhn)—a custom, idea, or belief passed down through time

unique (YOO-neek)—one of a kind

White House (WITE HOUSS)—the official residence of the president of the United States

READ MORE

Borgert-Spaniol, Megan. *Super Simple Thanksgiving Activities: Fun and Easy Holiday Projects for Kids.* Minneapolis: Abdo Publishing, 2018.

Dittmer, Lori. *Thanksgiving Day.* Mankato, MN: Creative Education, 2021.

Mavrikis, Peter. *The First Thanksgiving: Separating Fact from Fiction.* North Mankato, MN: Capstone Press, 2022.

INTERNET SITES

Britannica Kids: Thanksgiving
kids.britannica.com/kids/article/Thanksgiving/353852

History for Kids: The First Thanksgiving
historyforkids.net/the-first-thanksgiving.html

National Geographic Kids: The First Thanksgiving
kids.nationalgeographic.com/history/article/first-thanksgiving

Plimoth Patuxet Museums: For Students
plimoth.org/for-students

INDEX

ABOUT THE AUTHOR

Charles C. Hofer is a biologist, photographer, and writer living in southern Arizona. He is a regular contributor to several award-winning magazines, including *Muse* and *Ask*.